GROSS JOBS
Working with
FOOD

by Nikki Bruno

raintree

a Capstone company — publishers for children

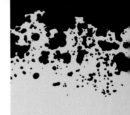

Raintree is an imprint of Capstone Global Library Limited, a company incorporated in England and Wales having its registered office at 264 Banbury Road, Oxford, OX2 7DY – Registered company number: 6695582

www.raintree.co.uk
myorders@raintree.co.uk

Edited by Hank Musolf
Designed by Bobbie Nuytten
Original illustrations © Capstone Global Library Limited 2019
Picture research by Heather Mauldin
Production by Katy LaVigne
Originated by Capstone Global Library Ltd
Printed and bound in India

ISBN 978 1 4747 7510 6
22 21 20 19 18
10 9 8 7 6 5 4 3 2 1

British Library Cataloguing in Publication Data
A full catalogue record for this book is available from the British Library.

Acknowledgements
We would like to thank the following for permission to reproduce photographs: Alamy: RichardBakerWork, 12, ZUMA Press Inc, 10-11; ASSOCIATED PRESS: Vaclav Pancer, 8-9; Getty Images: Dario Pignatelli/Bloomberg, 18-19, Nicola Tree,7; iStockphoto: andresr, 28-29, BanksPhotos, 24, carterdayne, 13, davidf, 22-23, Fertnig, cover, 1, FlairImages, 17, fotokostic, 14-15, IcemanJ, 8 (inset), Juanmonino, 25, PicturePartners, 16 (inset), proibu, 4-5, thaloengsak, 18 (inset); Shutterstock: David Tadevosian, 27, Kanghophoto, 20-21, Lamyai, 10 (inset), RossHelen, 6. Design Elements: Shutterstock: Alhovik, kasha_malasha, Katsiaryna Chumakova, Yellow Stocking.

CONTENTS

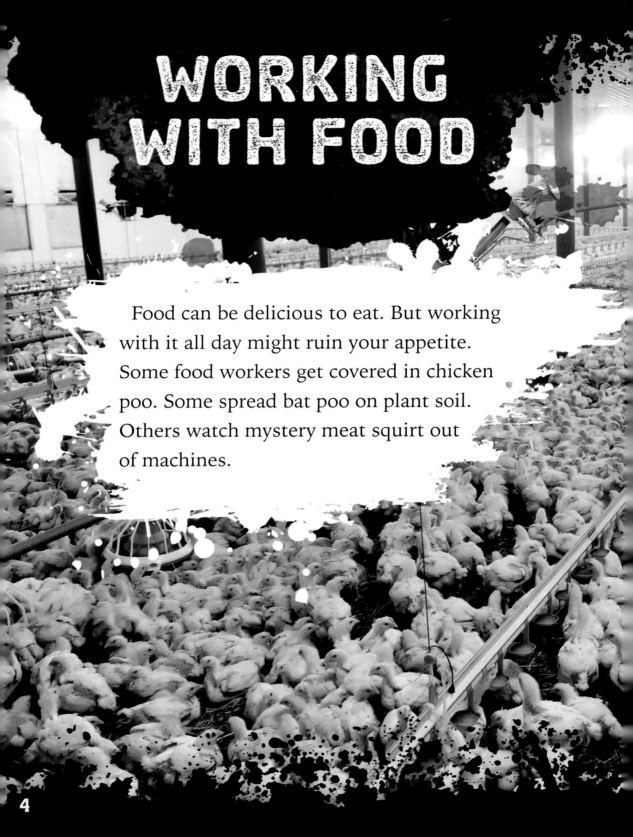

WORKING WITH FOOD

Food can be delicious to eat. But working with it all day might ruin your appetite. Some food workers get covered in chicken poo. Some spread bat poo on plant soil. Others watch mystery meat squirt out of machines.

BUTCHER

No one gets grosser or closer to your food than a butcher. Butchers cut dead animals into clean, neat packages of meat. They use knives, saws and meat grinders. It is a bloody, smelly, messy job.

GROSS-O-METER

DID YOU KNOW?

People in the United States eat the most meat per person in the world.

PET FOOD TASTER

Pet food tasters make sure pet food smells and tastes good enough for cats or dogs. These workers look at the food, smell it and, yes, even taste it. They also come up with new recipes. They use ingredients such as liver and crushed bone.

DID YOU KNOW?

Pet food tasters have to chew the food they test. But they do not have to swallow it.

GROSS-O-METER

RESTAURANT HEALTH INSPECTOR

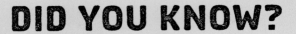

Health **inspectors** visit restaurants to make sure health and safety rules are followed. Inspectors have found dead rats and chicken poo in restaurants. One even found cat food in a fridge. The cook was using it in tuna sandwiches!

GROSS-O-METER

DID YOU KNOW?

Really good health inspectors can smell cockroaches. The bugs have an oily scent.

inspector person who checks or searches things

FISH GUTTER

The smell of one fish can be gross. Now multiply that fish by thousands. Fish gutters open and remove the insides of fish. This job is bloody and slippery. And the smell never goes away.

DID YOU KNOW?

Fish factory workers use little vacuum cleaners. The vacuum sucks out blood and other body fluids.

FERTILIZER SPREADER

Plants aren't very gross. But what they grow in can be nasty. Plants need a gas called **nitrogen**. Where do farmers find nitrogen? In cow, horse, sheep, pig and even bat poo! **Fertilizer** spreaders breathe in the smell of poo all day.

GROSS-O-METER

DID YOU KNOW?

Some companies use human poo to make fertilizer. Machines turn sewage sludge into fertilizer.

nitrogen colourless, odourless gas
fertilizer substance used to make crops grow better

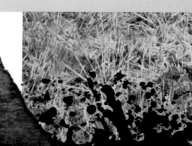

CHEESEMAKER

Cheese is basically spoiled milk. Cheesemakers use waste from **bacteria** to separate milk's solids from its liquids. They take the solid pieces called **curds** and cook them. The chunky pieces are pressed together into cheese.

MOULD: THE SECRET INGREDIENT!

GROSS-O-METER

Some cheesemakers actually *want* **mould** in their cheese! Mould makes blue cheese creamy and flavourful. Cheesemakers sprinkle some cheeses with mould. The mould gives it a white skin.

bacteria very small living things that exist all around you and inside you; some bacteria cause disease

curd solid part of spoiled milk; it can be eaten or turned into cheese

mould fuzzy substance that sometimes grows on old food

CHICKEN NUGGET MAKER

Kids alone eat thousands of chicken nuggets every day. But few people love working in nugget factories. Ground-up chicken parts squirt out through machines. This mixture might contain muscle, blood vessels, crushed bone, **nerves** and fat.

GROSS-O-METER

DID YOU KNOW?

Some fast-food chicken nugget brands are made of only half meat. The other half has other chicken parts, such as ground-up bone and fat.

nerve thin fibre that carries messages between the brain and other parts of the body

ANT EGG HARVESTER

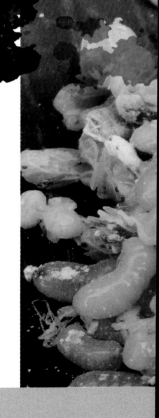

Beef or beans are common on tacos. But some people in Mexico fill tacos with ant eggs! The eggs are high in protein. Ant egg harvesters have to collect the eggs.

GROSS-O-METER

DID YOU KNOW?

Ants attack the egg harvesters while they work. The workers have to shake the ants off without hurting them.

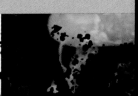

PIG FARMER

Millions of people love bacon. But they probably wouldn't love raising the pigs it comes from. Pigs are muddy and very smelly. They eat food called slop. Pig farms have huge ponds filled with pig poo and wee.

GROSS-O-METER

DID YOU KNOW?

Sometimes pig waste ponds explode. This happens after **methane** gas builds up.

methane colourless, flammable gas produced by the decay of plant and animal matter

DISH WASHER

A delicious meal at a restaurant ends in the kitchen sink. Dish washers must clean this mess. Imagine towers of crusty plates. Half-eaten food clings to forks and spoons. The smells mix together in a soggy mess.

DID YOU KNOW?

Restaurant dish washers use strong hoses. The water from the hose sometimes sprays old food back into the dish washer's face.

SAUSAGE MAKER

What are the grossest parts of an animal?
You can find them in sausage. Sausage
is a mixture of ground-up meat. Some
sausages include blood and organ meats.
The mixture is squirted into a **casing**.
Some casings are made of **intestines**.

GROSS-O-METER

DID YOU KNOW?

Some sausage is mostly made of blood. It is called blood sausage. Blood sausage is popular in many countries. Each country has their own version of blood sausage. It may look gross, but many people think it's delicious!

casing thin, skin-like layer that keeps sausage together
intestine long tube that carries and digests food and stores waste products; it is divided into the small intestine and large intestine

THANK YOU FOOD WORKERS!

Food workers grow, make and process the world's food. They often get dirty and smelly in the process. These people help us stay healthy and fill our stomachs. They get gross to keep our food tasty and safe.

GLOSSARY

bacteria very small living things that exist all around you and inside you; some bacteria cause disease

casing thin, skin-like layer that keeps sausage together

curd solid part of spoiled milk; it can be eaten or turned into cheese

fertilizer substance used to make crops grow better

inspector person who checks or searches things

intestine long tube that carries and digests food and stores waste products; it is divided into the small intestine and large intestine

methane colourless, flammable gas produced by the decay of plant and animal matter

mould fuzzy substance that sometimes grows on old food

nerve thin fibre that carries messages between the brain and other parts of the body

nitrogen colourless, odourless gas

FIND OUT MORE

BOOKS

Farmer (Diary of a…), Angela Royston
(Raintree, 2014)

From Field to Plate (Source to Resource), Michael Bright
(Wayland, 2016)

Nasty Nature (Horrible Science), Nick Arnold
(Scholastic, 2018)

WEBSITES

www.bbc.com/bitesize/guides/zf6fr82/revision/1
Learn more about where your food comes from.

www.bbc.com/bitesize/clips/zmsjmp3
Learn more about health and safety in food production.

INDEX